HOW TO CREATE POWE POWERPOINT 2010 PRESENTATION EASILY:
BASICS FOR BEGINNERS
Joan Mullally
Evelyn Trimborn

I0004848

If you're thinking about buying or already own PowerPoint 2010 but are not sure if you can master the skills to create powerful presentations, this illustrated step-by-step "quick start" guide is designed to help you create and deliver impressive, high-quality presentations to your target audience.

Go step-by-step through the process of creating a full-featured PowerPoint presentation quickly and easily. Learn how to:

+Create a new deck
+Format slides
+Add text
+Add images
+Use animation to get your points across
+Engage the attention of your audience through the strategic choices that you make on each slide

and much more.

Discover how to:
+use your presentations to expand your brand
+increase your number of prospective customers and clients
+structure your presentations to command attention no matter what the length is of your speaking engagement or meeting.
+use your decks to market your business on some of the most popular sites on the Internet
+make videos to market your business, even if you're camera shy

and much more.

Follow the steps in this guide to create your first PowerPoint 2010 deck so you can use it a variety of ways to both market your business and bring in extra income. Get top tips on how to create powerful professional-looking PowerPoint presentations that will impress and pave your path to success.

If you're eager to add more visual content such as presentations and video to your website, blog and other marketing activities, grab this guide today and start using PowerPoint as both a promotional tool and a whole new path to profitability.

ABOUT THE AUTHORS

Joan Mullally and Evelyn Trimborn have been marketing online for nearly 20 years and are the authors of more than 100 business and marketing titles designed to help new business owners gain the skills they need to succeed. They have both worked as PowerPoint specialists.

REVIEWS

5 stars - Excellent
This guide lives up to its title. I opened it on my Kindle reader or my Smartphone and followed the instructions as I worked on my desktop computer in Powerpoint. Never did a presentation in my life and managed to wow everyone who saw it, because they all asked for copies of it after I gave my talk. Would definitely recommend.

5 stars-Exactly what I needed
Powerpoint is one of those computer programs you really need to use in order to get any good at it. But with so many features, it can be confusing to even know where to begin in terms of dos and don'ts. In this guide, it is clear the authors know exactly how to use the program for marketing businesses, delivering educational presentations, and more. There is no fluff and plenty of guidance. I followed along on my Smartphone and was able to bang out 3 decks in only a couple of hours. I had all the info, but I needed to make it look great. Thanks to this guide, it did. My boss was so impressed he wanted me to teach him how to do HIS decks too! 2 thumbs up for sure.

5 stars-Perfect for any busy marketer
These days, you have to learn so many programs in order to get your job done as an online marketer. Everything I needed to know to create a great marketing deck for my online business was right here. I read it on my Kindle and all the step by step instructions with the handy screenshots and my own drop down menus means I am now making great-looking decks for the business and for presentation sharing sites. This is a hands-on book, not something you can just flip through the pages of. Excellent-very useful at a great price.

HOW TO CREATE POWERFUL POWERPOINT 2010 PRESENTATIONS QUICKLY AND EASILY

BASICS FOR BEGINNERS

Joan Mullally
Evelyn Trimborn

Eternal Spiral Books

COPYRIGHT 2011-2016 by the authors.
All rights reserved.
Seventh edition 2016 with all new material.

ISBN-13: 978-1540827258
ISBN-10: 1540827259

Published by Eternal Spiral Books
New York, New York
http://EternalSpiralBooks.com

Eternal Spiral Books is pleased to publish a variety of guides to help you transform your life through practical action steps. Topics include finance, health, marketing, self-help, and small business.

Please visit us online for the latest titles, and a free newsletter, free articles and more. http://EternalSpiralBooks.com/newsletter

Lend to a Friend: Did you know you can lend books on your Kindle? We at Eternal Spiral Books encourage this so that you can share this guide with family and friends to help them transform their lives as well. To learn more, go to Kindle Lending http://www.amazon.com/gp/help/customer/display.html/?ie=UTF8& camp=1789&creative=390957&linkCode=ur2&nodeId=200549320 &tag=esb1012-20

All of our titles are also available through the Kindle Unlimited program-more than 1 million books to read for 1 low monthly fee.

DISCLAIMER

This guide is designed for general advice only. It is not a substitute for advice given by a qualified professional with respect to your own individual business and financial circumstances or any taxation or legal issues. You should never delay in seeking professional help because of anything you might have read in this or any other guide, website and so on.

PowerPoint® is a trademarked name. The trademark symbol should be implied throughout.

Note: Whenever possible, we have tried to get the images as clear as possible. However, on occasion there is a dropdown menu that blinks on and off and can't be held open long enough for a copy to be made, so we have had to use screen grab software, which does not always render the best quality. You should be able to follow along via the text even if the image isn't totally perfect. Thanks for your understanding.

We have also left white space in this book so you can make notes as you follow along step by step. This is not a 'quick read' kind of book, but rather, an action guide you can use to create high-quality PowerPoint presentations over and over again.

Once you have created one, you will become better and better at this invaluable business and marketing skill.

DEDICATION

To all our readers. You inspire us every day!

And to our families, for their love and support, which makes our crazy writing schedules possible.

And to our dogs. There's nothing quite like the joy of rescue dogs.

PREFACE TO THE SEVENTH EDITION

As with all our titles, we review them once a year to make sure they are current in terms of links and information, and update them as needed. The exciting new developments at SlideShare, for example, are important for anyone who wishes to use the site to market their business effectively.

With the world of the Internet constantly changing, we have also removed old links and added new ones, to help you get as much out of this guide as possible.

Finally, we love to hear from readers with any questions they may have, to make this guide as useful as possible to complete beginners, and add new material as needed.

Here's wishing you the best of success in creating powerful and profitable PowerPoint presentations.

TABLE OF CONTENTS

INTRODUCTION

PowerPoint® presentations for business purposes have become an almost essential element of any meeting, seminar or webinar. From marketing a business to keeping in touch with family and friends, everyone is now using presentation software to create attractive multimedia displays.

PowerPoint® has become almost a global standard when it comes to designing powerful presentations. It was originally a stand-alone program, and quite expensive. Now you can usually buy it as part of the Microsoft Office Suite of programs.

There are other presentation programs available, but one of the biggest advantages of using PowerPoint is that the menus (sometimes referred to as ribbons) on the top of the page in the 2010 version of the program bear strong similarities to the menus in Microsoft Word, which has also become an almost global standard for word processing.

In this guide, we will review the essentials for creating powerful PowerPoint 2010 presentations that look professional without you needing to spend hours of your time creating them. Once you create your decks, you will be able to use them for a variety of business purposes, including, but not limited to:

+ In-Person Presentations:
  * Meetings
  * Conferences
  * Seminars

+ Online presentations:
  * Webinars
  * Videos on video-sharing websites like YouTube
  * Part of a Camtasia video of your desktop

+ Downloadable files:
  * A self-contained presentation that will play on any computer

* A PDF file of all of the slides in your deck to use as teaching materials
* A PDF file of your deck for people to use to take notes while you are presenting in person or live
* A PDF file that people can print and use as a checklist of action steps in relation to the content presented.

Since we all work in the marketing and technology worlds, we will be focusing mainly on how to create a PowerPoint presentation for business purposes. Once you understand the main principles and become familiar with the menus in the 2010 version of the program, you will definitely find many other uses for this powerful but easy-to-use software.

Before we get started, we need to have a few essentials in place:
1-PowerPoint 2010 installed on your computer
2-An outline of what you would like to present on each slide of your presentation
3-Content for each slide, such as text and images that you can copy and paste into your presentation

Once you have these three items, you can get started with this guide. One other final thing to note before we continue is that the screenshots in this guide are from PowerPoint 2010 and designed as a step by step tutorial you can use to create your own deck. So, now that we have the prerequisites out of the way, it is time to start creating your first PowerPoint presentation.

CHAPTER 1: HOW TO CREATE POWERPOINT SLIDES

Step 1: Start a New Presentation

When you open PowerPoint, you will be presented with a new title slide. If you are not, you will need to click File and then click New. This will bring up the first blank slide in your presentation:

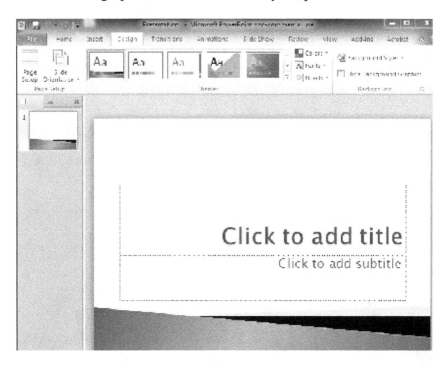

Step 2: Select a Theme

Click the Design tab and you should see a screen similar to the one below. This tab allows you to select a theme from several design choices and color options. Using the slider or bottom arrow in the center of the screenshot, you can scroll through the available themes. As you mouse over each theme, you will get a preview of what it will look like. page. Select the theme based on the layout you want rather than the color scheme. You can customize the colors later once you have chosen your theme. The main consideration is that a light background with dark text will be much easier to read, especially for people who might be at the back of the room when you are presenting.

Here is another screenshot of some of the themes available:

Select the theme of your choice by clicking on the icon. It will then bring up your first slide.

Step 3: Edit Theme

Once you have chosen your theme, it will be time to edit it. You can change the color, fonts and effects by using the drop-down arrows as indicated in the Design tab image below:

In the next screen shot, you can see the many color choices available, clustered together into complementary groupings. Try several until you find one that matches your business logo or the style of your business, such as formal versus informal. Try to make all of your marketing materials look similar to one another to help brand your business effectively.

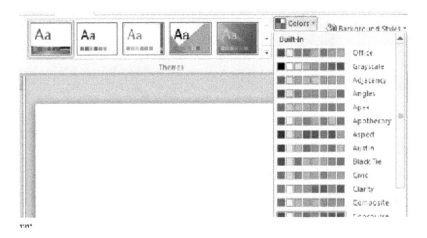

Now that you have chosen your theme and colors, you can change the background if you wish. On the Design tab, using the drop-down arrow next to Background Styles, mouse over your options to get a preview of what features each option will give you:

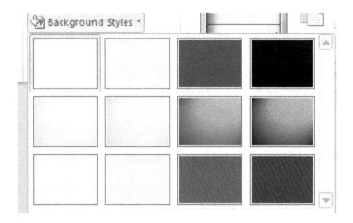

Each theme will come with its own set of background options, from plain white, to fades and subtle designs. You can also change the fonts and effects from the Design tab as well. Those options are located directly below the colors option. Scroll through your various choices until you find the font and the background that you like.

Step 4: Edit Title Page

Now that you have the presentation design you want, it is time to start editing and adding other features to the slides. As indicated in the slide image below, you simply need to click the area in the slide to copy and paste or type in text:

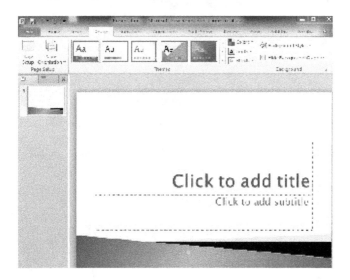

Switching back to the Home tab will give you editing features as in Word. You can add underlining, bolding, or italics. You can change the font, create bullets and more:

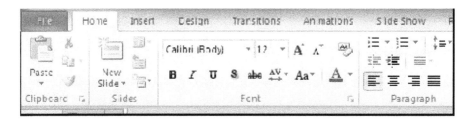

Each slide will also have an area at the bottom to add notes if you wish. This can be handy to help prompt you about anything you don't wish to forget to talk about in relation to each slide in your deck.

The first slide you create will be your title slide. Name your presentation:

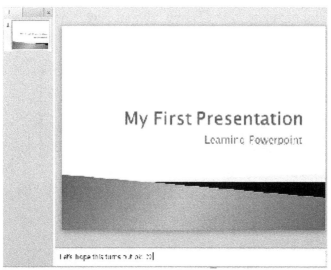

Name it using keywords and then save it. Keywords will help you find it when you need to on your computer, and will make it more searchable on search engines and slideshow sharing sites like SlideShare.

Step 5: Add Slide # 2

To add another slide, navigate to the Home tab and click Slide to create new blank slide:

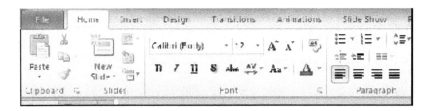

Click the drop-down arrow below the New Slide icon to bring up other types of slide options:

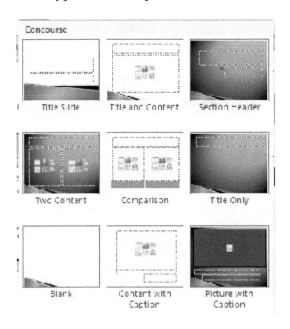

As you can see, there are a number of different formats. The main once you will be using will be the title slide, title with text, and title with 2 columns. They are easy to edit and ideal for ensuring your presentation will not look too cluttered. Click the slide format of your choice. Then just click on the slide to enter your text. You can type in your text, or copy and paste it in.

Step 6: Create additional slides by repeating Step 5 for each slide you wish to add. To move between slides, simply click the slide in the left-hand sidebar that you wish to view and/or edit:

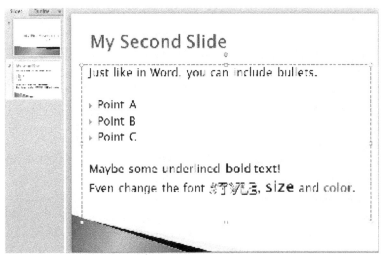

You can also re-order the slides in the deck by dragging and dropping the thumbnails on the left.

Insert the text you have prepared into each slide. Don't make the slides too crowded or the text too small. You can always add another slide.

Now that you have created a new deck and added slides and content, it is time to start making it look more attractive by adding media to your slides.

CHAPTER 2: HOW TO INSERT MEDIA INTO PRESENTATION SLIDES

Once you have created the text slides that you wish, you can add media to them to liven up your presentation and give it a more sophisticated style. Good graphics should be relevant and have real impact upon the audience to support your message. These days, everyone expects good images to support text. Gather any images and video to insert on the slides into a folder so you can find what you need easily as we go through the action steps in this chapter.

You can get good images from stock photography sites, public domain sites and royalty-free sites. Avoid anything copyrighted. You can also always use your digital camera to take images you can use in your marketing materials.

When choosing images, make sure they go along with your color scheme and style you want to convey in your marketing materials.

Once you have all of your images organized, you can start to insert your pictures. Take a few moments to organize your images into a folder for your deck and when you are ready, move on to Step 1.

Step 1: Insert Pictures

There are two ways to insert media into your slides. The first is that when a new slide opens, before you add any text, you can click the appropriate icon in the middle of the slide:

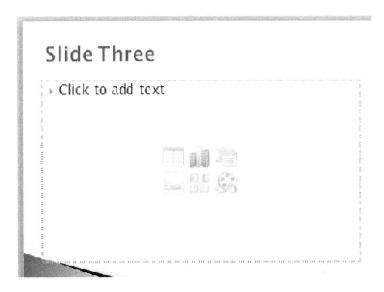

The choices, from left to right on the top row are a table, chart, or a smart graphic. The choices on the bottom row are an image, clip art, or a video.

The second way is by using the Insert menu. Here you have the option of inserting all types of images, shapes, tables, charts, text boxes, video, equations and more into your slides:

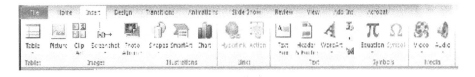

First, we are going to show you how to add an image. To do this, click the picture icon on the Insert tab, which will bring up the pictures library on your computer. If the image you want to use is not located in the Image Library, simply navigate to the folder where you have stored the media for the presentation you are creating. Select the image you wish to add, and then click the Open button as shown below:

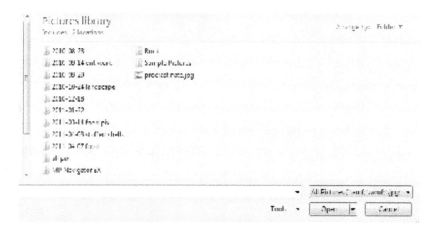

This will insert the image into your slide. If you click the image, you will see that it brings up a selection box around it. Drag the side or corner of the selection box to make the image larger or smaller. To place it where you wish, click on the image once and hold the left mouse button down. Then drag and drop the image wherever you wish on the slide.

Slide Three

Clicking on the image that you have placed on the slide will also open a Picture Tools tab. In this menu, you can edit the image further:

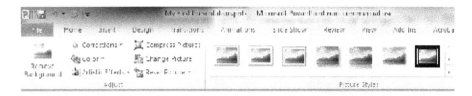

For example, the menu on the right offers a variety of frame effects to put around your image in order to make it stand out on the slide. The choice on the far right is to put a heavy black box around the image. If we continue to look at the rest of the menu over to the right of the black box, we see that you can choose the picture border in terms of color, thickness, dashed or solid lines, and the weight or heaviness of the lines:

In our example, we have moved our image to the left side of the slide, and inserted a text box (from the Insert tab, the icon that says Text box in the center of the page) so we can add our text on the right of the image:

Slide Three

Procrastination is often the result of one of the following:

- **Fear** Of failure or success

- **Perfectionism** We expect too much of ourselves

- **Time** Too much work, not enough time

Today, we'll be discussing how to recognize when you're procrastinating and what to do to overcome it.

If you have chosen a 2-column slide format, insert text in one and the image in the other.

Step 2: Inserting Video

You can insert video into your PowerPoint presentations as well. To do this, navigate to the Insert tab and click Video on the far right:

Navigate to the location of the video you want to insert, which should be in the folder where you have gathered all your media for your presentation at the start of this chapter. Select the video and click the Insert button.

Note: If the video is already online, use the drop-down arrow on the Insert button and select Link to File, then enter the URL of the video file. This will keep the size of the PowerPoint file small. YouTube is one of the best places to upload your videos. Once they are uploaded, you can embed links at your site, in your social media account, and more.

Want to keep your videos relative private? when uploading, choose the Private or Unlisted option. You can also close the comments so nothing negative shows on your video page.

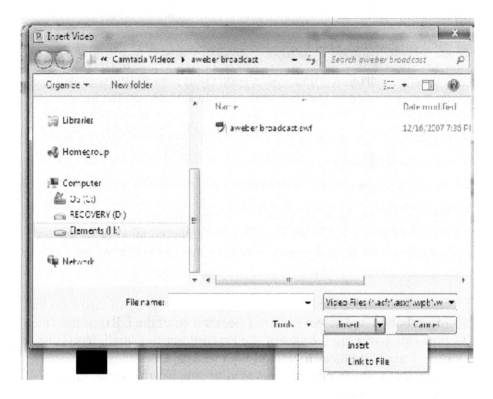

Once you click Insert, your video will be inserted into the slide. You can move it around as you did the image in Step 1, using the arrows tool to position it as you wish. The following is an example of the way it will appear within your deck:

Using Aweber

This video shows you how to send a broadcast
through the Aweber autoresponder service.

You can also click the Video Tools tab to edit the video shape, give
it a border and add other effects to enhance the appearance of the
slide:

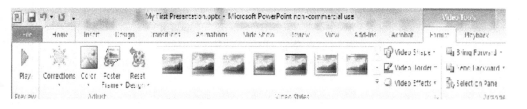

Step 3: Insert Charts

Bar charts and other types of graphical depictions of data are usually quite helpful for presenting marketing material. If you already have a chart you have created in Excel that you would like to add, you can do so by clicking the Insert tab then selecting Charts:

Select the type of chart you'd like to insert and click OK:

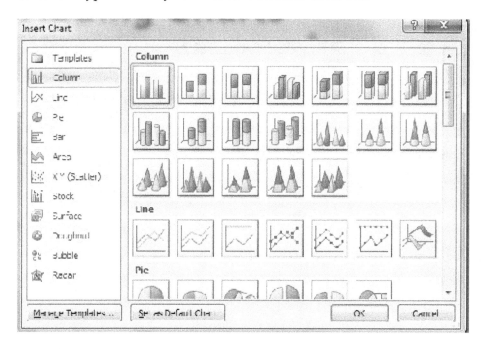

Once the chart data has been inserted, you can click it to open the Chart Tools. Here you will be able to change the chart colors, edit the data and more:

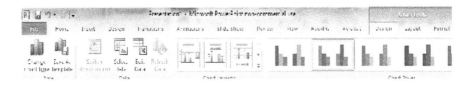

Make the changes as needed, and SAVE.

Step 4: Insert Tables

Tables are another way to organize your data conveniently. To insert a table, click the Insert tab, and then click Table. Using your mouse, highlight to select how many rows and columns you want the table to include:

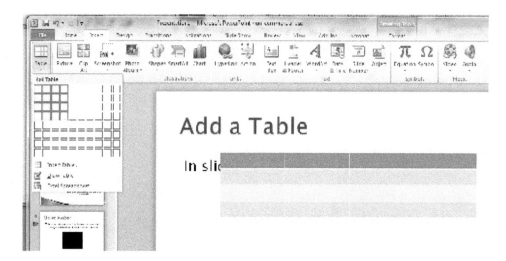

Move the table as you did the image and video, positioning it where you wish on the slide. To edit the table, simply click each cell and enter the data. Clicking the table once will also bring up the Table Tools, where you can change the layout, colors, borders, shading and more:

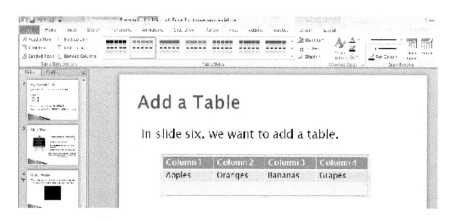

Again, you can add many elements to your slides to make them as fancy or detailed as you wish. Simply follow the steps as outlined above and look through the menu to explore all options available.

Step 5: Inserting Other Objects

In this step, we will look at the Insert menu in more detail. There is a close-up screen shot of the options on the left side of the Insert tab:

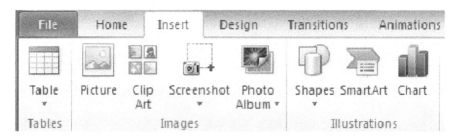

In this chapter, we have already discussed inserting an image in Step 1, Video in Step 2, Chart in Step 3 and Table in Step 4. Screenshot is a self-explanatory choice. Your computer will give you the option to insert an image of any windows that are open at the time that you are preparing your deck. A photo album is a set of images that you can create through the menu that pops up:

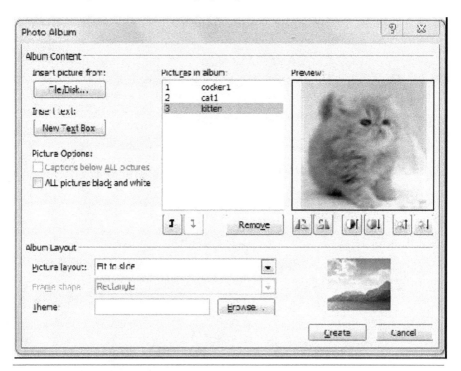

This is a photo album of pet photos that Evelyn is creating for her animal rescue work. You can see that there are three images, cocker1, cat and kitten. The photo showing is the third choice, kitten.

On the top left, you can see the two choices for creating the photo album, either to choose a photo from a file or disk, or insert text for a new text box. The images can be edited right in the photo album by clicking the choices under the image.

You can also lay out the album using the drop-down choices on the left, such as Fit to Slide. Depending on your choice of layout, you can edit the shape of the photos to create more interesting or dramatic effects.

Once you click the Create button on the lower right, your album will appear as a set of slides with the usual thumbnail navigation down the left-hand side of the page:

As you can see, there are several dog and cat images in the following photo album. Just click on the thumbnail of your choice to edit the image and its position on the page. Use the arrows to position it, re-size it and edit each image as needed until you are happy with your photo album. Then click Save.

When you click on Clip Art, you will see the second image on the next page appear on the right-hand side of your screen: These were the results when we entered the word "chart". Click on the image you wish to insert into your presentation and it will appear on the slide. Use the arrow tools to place it, re-size it and so forth.

The Shapes button produces this menu of choices:

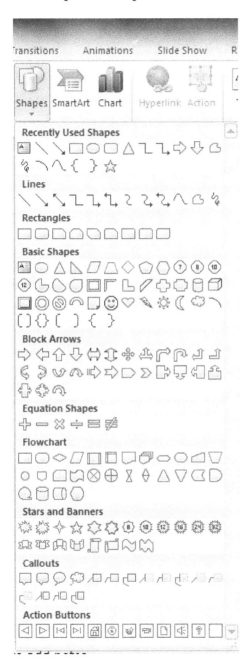

Click to add the shape of your choice. As you can see, there are a wide variety of choices, and you can edit the colors and features of these items as well.

For example, you can set how thick the outline of the shape should be, choose a solid line or dotted, the color of the outline, and the color inside the object. If you click on the shape, you will see all of your menu choices along the ribbon at the top. Adjust as needed to create the exact kinds of effects you want for the shape.

As a short-cut, you might can use some of the pre-prepared SmartArt and customize it rather than starting from scratch. The SmartArt menu choice will give you pre-formed diagrams that to edit by clicking on the text boxes on top of each element to label them. When you click on the button, a window with an extensive list of choices will appear:

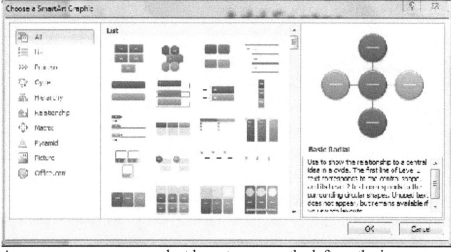

As you can see, you can select by category on the left, or the image icon in the center. When you click on the image icon, you will see a preview and description on the right. These elements can give your presentation an extremely professional-looking polish, and all you have to do is label each element of the graphic. Choose the color scheme that suits your business and deck best by going to the Design tab and clicking Choose Colors in the middle of the ribbon.

You can edit the text in each object by clicking on the center, or on the image by clicking on the outer border of the image.

We have already seen the Chart menu, but here it is again to remind ourselves:

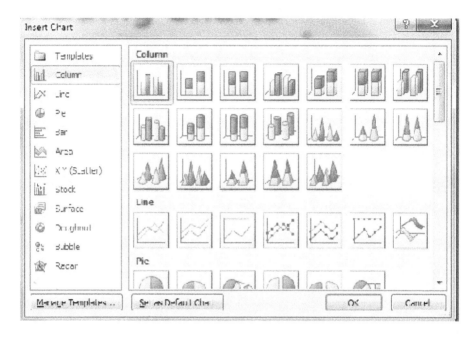

Step 6: Inserting More Objects

Moving over towards the right-hand side of the Insert menu, you will see:

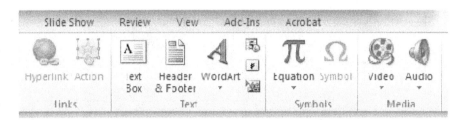

You can add other text boxes to the slides in addition to the ones already given to you. For example, if you wanted to create a number of small text boxes as captions for your images, or break up the text in order to vary the appearance of the slides in your deck, you can do so:

A text box can be added anywhere you wish on the slide

This is useful for creating captions and other textual effects.

Pay particular attention to the header and footer menu choice. Footers on the sides, such as page numbers and the name of your company, will help you create a unified-looking branded deck. This is the screen that will appear when you click on the header and footer button:

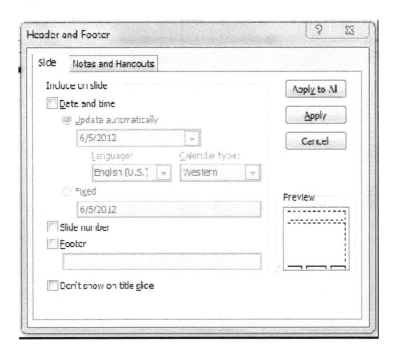

We suggest you insert a slide number and footer text for your company, and/or the title of the presentation. Note the check box at the bottom if you wish to not have your footer on the first slide of your presentation. Most people don't have the number on the first slide.

WordArt can help you make your title page and slides more attractive, and the menu that drops down gives you a range of choices:

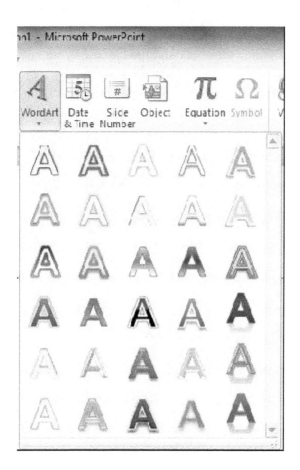

We have already discussed adding video, but here is the drop-down menu of choices that will appear when you click on the button:

Select your choice and then upload the file of your choice or the URL of the video that you want to embed. Keep in mind that you would need to have an Internet connection in order for the video to show while you were giving the presentation.

The Audio menu looks similar:

However, note the last choice on the menu. You can record custom audio for the slide when you click this choice by pressing the dark round circle on the right when you get to the next window. That is the Record button and will record your voice, music and so on.

Name the audio file you have created in order to save it. A play button icon will then appear on the slide so you can check the sound quality and duration of the audio file. If you make a mistake, you can simply delete the old file and start again. The audio record feature will work best if you have a high-quality microphone on your computer, but it will also work with your computer's regular microphone if you sit close enough to it and don't have too much noise in the room when you are recording.

Step 7: Polishing and Proofing your Slides

Now that we have covered all of the important elements on the Insert menu, you can go back to edit the slides you have created in order to add your multimedia. Start with Slide 1. Go through each slide to add the elements that you wish. If you do not have a lot of images, consider creating a chart or using SmartArt or WordArt to enhance your slides.

Once you have reviewed every slide, check over your work once again to ensure that it appears exactly as you wish. Move the text and images around as needed by clicking and dragging. Then review your material one more time to check for any spelling or grammatical errors.

Check the text and images in relation to the footer at the bottom of the page to make sure nothing is overlapping. Click and use the arrows to move the footer and page number as needed, or move the images or re-size the text if you have to.

You can also move the text higher or lower on a page, but not too high or it will look a bit strange. If the slide can't be read easily because the font is too small, consider breaking up the text to add it to another slide. In this case, go to the slide menu for new slides and click Duplicate slide at the bottom of the menu. It will create another slide just below the first one. Break up the text on both slides so all the content is there but looks less crowded.

Next, look at the cover page of your slide. Make sure it is a good introduction to your presentation. Some people like to put a graphic above the title.

To conclude your presentation in a professional way, add a last slide which provides your contact information such as email address in case anyone has any questions about your presentation. They will also be able to contact you to follow up. If you wish, you can also offer people a copy of the deck if they email you. This is a good way to build an in-house email marketing list of people who have attended your marketing events and are interested in your marketing message. Tell them to contact you at the above address to ask for the deck and to be put onto your free newsletter list.

Once you are sure your presentation is polished and proofed, it will be time to add more interesting elements to your PowerPoint deck. Let's look at your options in the next chapter.

CHAPTER 3: ADD ANIMATION TO YOUR POWERPOINT PRESENTATIONS

To keep your audience interested as you go through your deck of slides, you can add animation to liven up your presentation. There are many options for animating text and images. This demonstration will walk you through the basics that will look tasteful and professional, not silly. You will need the a PowerPoint presentation previously started. You might wish to create a copy just in case you want one without animation, and one with.

Step 1: Animate Your Images

If you would like an image you have used to gradually come onto the screen in your presentation, you can animate the image. Select the image you wish to animate by going to the correct slide and clicking on the image. We have chosen to animate the image in slide # 3. You can tell we have selected it because the selection box is visible around the image:

Slide Three

Procrastination is often the result of one of the following:

- **Fear** – Of failure or success

- **Perfectionism** – We expect too much of ourselves

- **Time** – Too much work, not enough time

Today, we'll be discussing how to recognize when you're procrastinating and what to do to overcome it.

Click the Animations menu tab in the center of your screen to reveal your ribbon of choices:

The first choice on the ribbon is Preview, which will allow you to see what the effect is of the changes you make on each slide. Then you will see an Animation list going from left to right. None is the default, that is, no animation. The other choices will create various effects when you click on then, such as Appear, Fade, Fly In, Float in, Split, or Wipe. Appear will make it pop up, and Split will make it appear like sliding doors opening and closing.

To the right of these choices is another section of the menu:

Add Animation will give you more choices than the ones sitting on the ribbon when you first look at it. You can also scroll down from the ribbon using the arrow on the right to see all these choices:

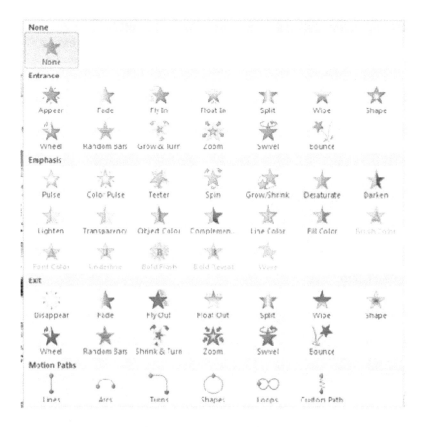

Note that there are three main categories for your effects:
* Entrance
* Emphasis
* Exit

and one category for Motion Paths.

You can set all these effects for one object if you so choose. The object can be sitting on the screen (NONE) or can slide in from the right or left if you animate it. It can get highlighted for emphasis, and then depart from the screen in various ways, from completely disappearing (Vanish) to Bouncing out. This can make your presentations very lively and interesting, but too much of a good thing can ruin the effect.

Plus, some effects can be quite comical, such as Bounce. Choose your animations baed on the formality of the deck you are creating and the overall style and tone of your business and presentation.

You will also notice a list of Motion Paths at the bottom from which to choose. You can therefore set the direction and motion of your items so that they are not always in a straight line. Again, this is an effect that you should use judiciously for emphasis, and not on every slide, or things will start to get a bit too cluttered and busy.

Underneath Motion Effects, you will see:

More Entrance Effects...

More Emphasis Effects...

More Exit Effects...

More Motion Paths...

For each of the choices you see in the main menu, there are submenus:

Entrance Effects

If you click the option More Entrance Effects at the bottom of the menu, you will see this:

Note that you have a choice of Basic, Subtle, Moderate and Exciting. This will be the same for the next two menus.

Emphasis Effects

The Emphasis Effects menu looks this way:

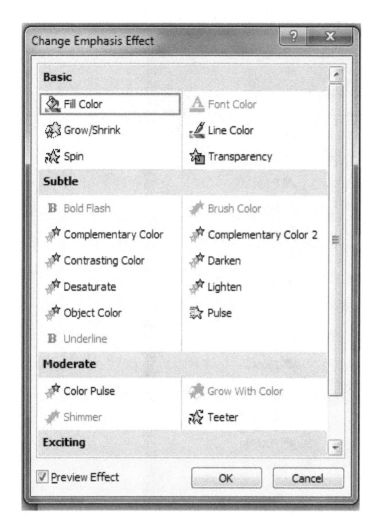

Exit Effects

The Exit Effects menu looks like this:

Motion Paths

The Motion Paths menu looks this way:

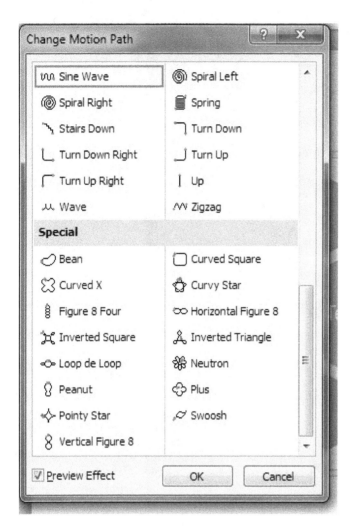

The small drawing next to each choice indicates what motion the image will take on the page. Note that you have a choice of categories; Basic, Lines and Curves, and Special. With the help of these paths, your image can move all around the screen, doing figure eights, zig-zags and so on. This can be useful, impressive, or comical depending on the path and the timing of the path.

Note that each effect can also be timed, that is, how long it takes for it to appear, move, disappear and so on. You might time it for a split second, like 0.25 seconds, or longer, such as 2 to 4 seconds, to give you time as you are transitioning from one slide or topic to the next. You can use the menu at the top right:

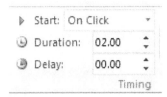

Or, if you have extensive changes, you can click on Animation Pane on the top towards the right on the ribbon:

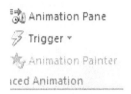

When you click on this choice, you will see a pane open up on the left that looks like this:

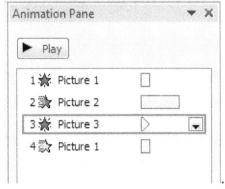

Click on the image number of the items that you have animated to refine your selections. Depending on what effect you have chosen, you will see a menu similar to this:

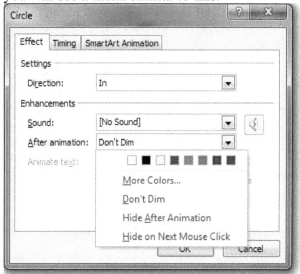

The choices of tabs will usually be Effect and Timing, and SmartArt Animation, depending upon what effect you have chosen. As you can see from the example above, you can set the direction, In or Out, Sound when the image arrives on screen, and dimming effects and colors when the image is on screen.

You can also dim it and change colors as it goes off the screen. You can choose Hide After Animation or Hide on Mouse Click in this menu, to make the image disappear as you choose.

Once you have created all of the images on your slide and animated them as you wish, they will be numbered on your page, with a corresponding number on your Animation Pane on the right. To edit the animation, click on the number in the pane that corresponds to the item you have created:

As you can see, the dog animation was created third on the page. You can also see here that when we click on Number 3 in our Animation Pane, we will get this menu. If we toggle the sound effect menu, we can see an alphabetical list of options. Depending on what kind of effect you are creating in your overall presentation, you can choose a sound such as Bomb or Breeze. Again, beware of the style and tone of the deck you are trying to create when choosing a sound.

On the second tab, Timing, you can set the timing of the event and how long it lasts:

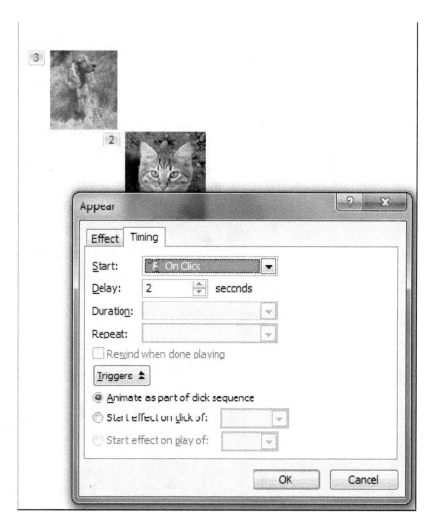

In most cases, you should start the movement on click, because you will be clicking to advance from one slide to the next. Within each slide, you can click several times to make each element on the slide appear, headline, text boxes, and of course images, as we have been discussing. If you don't set the On click option, the slideshow will continue to run on its own, which might be too fast for you as you are presenting. It can be a pain to stop, find your place, and restart, so the on click option is best.

You might want to set a delay so that the effect is not too abrupt, and you can also set the duration of the effect. The default is two seconds, but if you want a slower fade in or fly in, you might slow it down to four or five seconds, so that your cocker spaniel image does not race on screen like a greyhound.

You can also sequence all of the fade ins and outs on the page in order to get all of the objects on and off screen in the correct order.

So let's look at our specific example again. In this part of the guide, we decided on the image Split effect, in which the two sections of our procrastination image will come together. In the image below, you can see the two sides coming together from the outside edges into the center of the image, like elevator doors closing:

Slide Three

Procrastination is often the result of one of the following:

- Fear – Of failure or success

- Perfectionism – We expect too much of ourselves

- Time – Too much work, not enough time

Today, we'll be discussing how to recognize when you're procrastinating and what to do to overcome it.

If we look at the middle of our menu ribbon now, we can see that next to the Add Animation button, our Effect Options button has changed to indicate that the Split option comes with various choices:

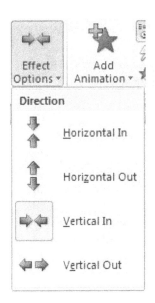

You can see that our choice was the Vertical In choice for our Procrastinator's image. The other three choices are indicated by the direction in which the arrows are pointing.

To summarize this step, you will be able to select animation effects for each image on each slide using the Add Animation option and choosing from among the three main categories of choices:
* Entrance
* Emphasis
* Exit

and Motion Paths.

For each of the three effects, you will have various options depending upon which effect you choose. You can access the options through the Effect Options menu.

To review all the choices you have made, refine them, or edit them, click on the Animation Pane button. The pane will open on the right of your screen and you will be able to click the number corresponding to the effect that you have created for each image that you have created. Once you click on a choice from the Animation Pane menu, you can refine that choice by using the Effect and Timing tabs.

You can animate both images and text. Just remember, you don't want every slide in the deck to be too busy looking. Simple is best, especially for an in-person business presentation. So let's look next at animating your text.

Step 2: Animating Text

You can animate text in the same way as images. However, with text, the whole text window will move. If you want to animate bullets individually, they would each have to have their own text box.

Hiding text can be useful if you want your audience to guess at some of the answers if you ask them a question. It adds a bit of interest and interactivity to your presentation.

In this case, you would animate it so the content appeared on click, bullet-by-bullet or paragraph-by-paragraph.

Using the deck you have already created, look through any slides you might wish to animate bullet by bullet. Duplicate the slide on the New Slide menu just to be on the safe side, and then create 1 text box for each bullet or paragraph. In the Animation navigation bar, use the drop-down arrow next to Effect Options to select how you want to animate the bullet or paragraph:

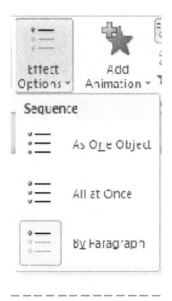

For example, if we wanted our bullets to zoom in or bounce into place, we would choose the By Paragraph option. Once the animation is applied, each element is assigned a number. You can click the number to change the animation for that particular paragraph. When you click on the number, the Animation Pane will appear on the right:

My Second Slide

Just like in Word, you can include bullets.

▸ Point A
▸ Point B
▸ Point C

Maybe some underlined **bold text!**
Even change the font STYLE, size and color.

You can apply more than one animation to an object. To do this, simply click the Add Animation button. Animations will play in the order in which they were applied, so you need to sequence them correctly. For example, if you have an entrance, emphasis and exit effect for each of three lines of text, you would need to order each entrance effect, then each emphasis, and then each exit to help keep things organized and flowing.

Number the image entrances 1, 2, 3, the emphases 4, 5, 6 and the exits 7, 8 9; unless you wanted them to appear, be emphasized, and then vanish, in which case you would have three numbers attached to the first image, 1, 2, 3, three to the second, 4, 5, 6, and then three to the third and final image on the slide, 7, 8, 9.

For each animation, click Add Animation and choose one effect, then the effect options. To refine all of your textual choices, move to Step 3.

Step 3: Using the Animation Pane for Text

To review all of the animations that you have created, click on the
Animation Pane:

The Animation Pane for the slide will open to the right. You can see
that each animation effect has an assigned number to the left. You
can change the animation effects, the timing and also play the entire
animation to see the way it will look once you are finished with your
edits:

Select a number or row in the menu. Note that the small icon next to
the number will give you an idea of what the effect is. They are color
coded: Green for Entrance, Yellow for Emphasis and Red for Exit.

You can set Point A, B and C as you like. When you have made all the changes for your effects and timing, click on Play to preview the effect on the slide and edit as needed.

Step 4: Choosing Your Effect Options

If you do not like the direction of certain effects, simply right-click the effect you wish to edit in the Animation Pane and select Effect Options. If the effect has an option, you will get a new menu for it. Note that not all effects will have extra options:

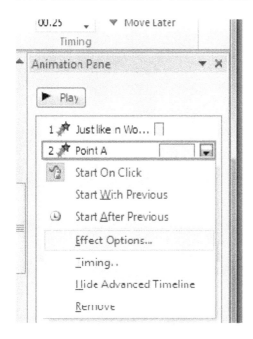

For example, you might click on Point A for your text's entrance animation effect. Let's imagine that this was a bullet point that you wanted to bounce into the presentation. With the effects option, you can enhance your animation by adding sound, a dimming feature, setting the timing and more. Simply make your selections and click OK when you are finished:

Step 5: Animation Timing

By default, the animation is set to play immediately upon the opening of the slide. To change when the animation begins to give it a time lag so that everyone can see your effects, select the effect in the Animation Pane. Then using the drop-down arrow next to the Start, choose when it should start: upon click, at the same time as the previous animation, or after the last animation:

You can edit the duration of the animation, as well as set a delay. These are measured in seconds, such as 2:00 seconds.

In addition, you can change the order in which the animations are applied. Simply click the effect in the Animation Pane and click the Move Earlier or Later arrow:

Summarizing Animations for Images and Text

These are the main effects that you can create for individual text and images. You do not have to animate every single item on every single slide. However, you want your audience to follow along as you discuss each bullet on your slide, or want to show some supporting data with an image that appears on screen when you click, this is an ideal way to accomplish this. You can add interest and interactivity by revealing answers or data in a strategic way. Animations can put you in charge of the material in a much more controlled way that simply showing one slide after the other. Since we are assuming you are using your deck for marketing purposes, careful use of animations can make a bit impact on your target audience.

Creating animated text and images is quite simple and can make your presentations really stand out. It can add interest and sometimes even a bit of fun to what might otherwise be a dull subject you need to present at work.

Step 6: Review Your Image and Text Animations for Each Slide

As we have said, you can set entrance, emphasis and exit animation for each image or paragraph of text. You should review each slide to see how it functions. Make notes as you view the slideshow as to anything you might wish to tweak.

Once you have reviewed each slide and have checked once more to make sure that everything is appearing as you wish, it will be time to put the finishing touches on the presentation and get ready to publish it. Let's look at these important topics in the next chapter.

CHAPTER 4: POWERPOINT TIMINGS, NARRATION AND PUBLISHING

This guide was created using PowerPoint 2010, which has the ability to publish a presentation as a movie file. This allows anyone to view it whether they have PowerPoint or not.

Before we publish our presentation, we first want to set the slide timing and add some narration to it. In order to accomplish this, you will need:

* PowerPoint 2010
* A complete presentation
* A microphone for your computer
* Speakers for your computer

You can use the built-in microphone on your computer, but for superior sound quality, get a reasonably-priced clip-on microphone, especially if you are planning to create a number of presentations to market your business. A good microphone is a must if you wish to start earning a new stream of income by hosting webinars and other live events, or offering online coaching. (See our guides on these 2 topics if you wish to learn more.) You can buy a good USB microphone for around $50.

The content on your slides should now be complete and proofread carefully. In our first step in this chapter, we will finish polishing the presentation in terms of slide transitions and timings.

Step 1: Set Slide Transitions and Timings

PowerPoint will automatically record your slide timings when you add narration. However, you can also manually adjust the timings if you prefer. To manually set these, look at the thumbnail navigation on the left-hand side of the screen. Click the slide you want to set the transition and timing for:

Click the Transitions tab at the top of your menus. This will give you options for how you want to transition from one slide to the next:

The choices are similiar to the options for animating text and images. The ribbon includes Cut, Fade, Push, Wipe, Split, Reveal, Random Bars and Shape. The icons will give you an idea of what the motion of the slide will be to reveal the entire slide to the audience when you click on it or it advances on its own according to the timings you have set. On click will give you more control.

Transitions are similar to Animations, except that Transitions affect the whole slide as it appears and then changes to the next slide, compared with Animations, which affect only individual images and paragraphs/bulleted items of text.

As you might expect, clicking on the arrow in the bottom right corner of the Transition to this Slide ribbon will reveal even more choices:

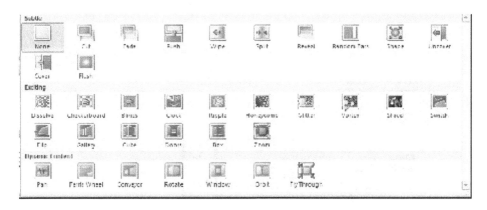

The choices are grouped under Subtle, Exciting and Dynamic Content. Subtle, as the name suggests, is not too dramatic, while the second row, Exciting, is much more 'in your face'.

Select the transition you would like for the slide you are currently on. Then go over to the right-hand side of your page. Under the Advanced Slide section on the top right, check the checkbox next to the word After.

Set the number of seconds you want the slide to take in order to appear on the screen. Here, we want it to show after 6 seconds when we click the mouse. This will give us a smooth transition from one slide to the next without it being too rapid and abrupt:

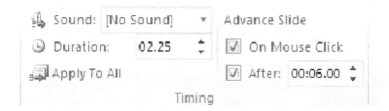

You will also notice we have selected the On Mouse Click option as well. This means the next slide will appear after 6 seconds when the mouse is clicked. You do not have to select the mouse click option; it's entirely up to you. If you want these same settings for all the slides, simply click Apply to All, next to the After box. Alternately, you can set each slide's timing individually. This will work well for slides that are more text heavy than others.

Note that the transition of slide timing would also be important if you wanted to make a movie in the .mp4 or other video format to upload to YouTube or other popular video sharing sites.

You can turn these timings off by going to the Slide Show tab and clicking Set Up Slide Show under the Set Up section:

Then click Advance slides and select Manual:

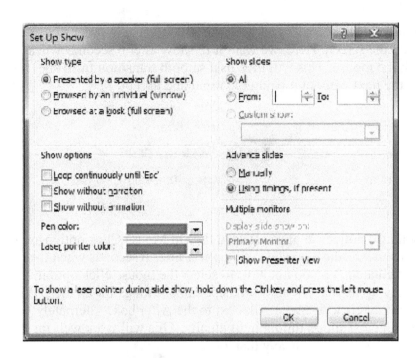

Note: This will NOT delete the timings. It will simply turn them off so you that you can manually advance the slides. To turn the timings back on, just navigate back to this area and click, "Use timings if present".

Step 2: Add Narration

In most cases you will be presenting your slideshow live. However, if you want to use it for marketing or educational purposes, such as a hosted webinar online, you might wish to add narration to your slide show so it can be viewed online any time.

You can also create decks to place in a members-only area for a coaching program, your consulting clients and so on. There are many ways to make money and marketing your business using your powerful PowerPoint presentations once you know how.

There are two ways to add narration to your slide show. The first is to record the narration when you create the slide show, before any live event in which you might be participating in or hosting. If you are going to record, leave about 5 seconds at the start of the recording because it has a tendency to lag and not record as soon as you start speaking.

The second way is to record it during a live presentation, which will allow you to include comments from your viewers in the recording. However, you may want to test this out a few times before your live event to ensure you are comfortable with how it works.

You also need to check that the sound quality is all you hope it will be if you intend to use the presentation for marketing purposes or as a paid product. In this case, you will want the audio to be as high-quality as possible. One way to ensure that everything can be heard is to repeat each question that is asked for the benefit of the entire audience. This is a good habit too because it gives you time to think of the best answer.

If you wish, you can also record questions and add them to the end of a second copy of the presentation, with answers and further slides. If you plan to do this, check the facilities provided for the location at which you will be speaking. Find out in advance if they will have microphones that can be passed around in order to clearly record the questions from the audience. If they do not, or you want to be sure that people can hear the question on your presentation recording, bring your own mike and repeat the question into it, then your answer.

If you hate your own voice, a third option is to write a script and hire a voice-over professional to record it onto your deck. Fiverr has a range of male and female voices and accents, such as American, English and Australia.

Listen to the samples they post at their pages to find ones that have the right voice and presentation style for your business, from light-hearted to serious. Prices start at around $5 per 100 words of script.

When reading their services offered description, be sure they will deliver a file of the completed deck at the end. Some will also give you the audio file as well if you wish to edit or use it for other purposes. Also make sure they are willing to give you at least 1 revision.

For the sake of this guide, we are going to demonstrate the first option, how to record the narrator prior to the event, not at the live event. PowerPoint will prompt you to record just the slide timings, just the narration, or both at the same time. If you are creating a presentation to play automatically on demand, perhaps as a message on your website, you will most likely want to record the narration and set the timing at the same time. This will ensure everything is in sync.

To start recording, click on the Slide Show tab. Then click the arrow next to Record Slide Show:

This will give you the option to record from beginning (the first slide) or record from current slide:

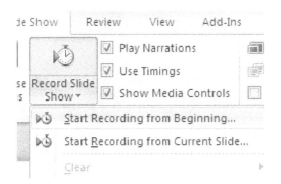

Once you make your selection, a dialog box will open. Select the narrations and laser pointer box. If you want it to automatically set the timings, select the slide and animation timings box as well. Otherwise, leave that box empty.

When you are ready, click "Start Recording":

To pause during narration, click Pause. To resume, click Resume Recording. When you're finished with the narration, right-click the slide and choose End Show.

Your recording and timings will automatically be saved and the slideshow will be visible in the slide sorter view with the timings listed below each slide:

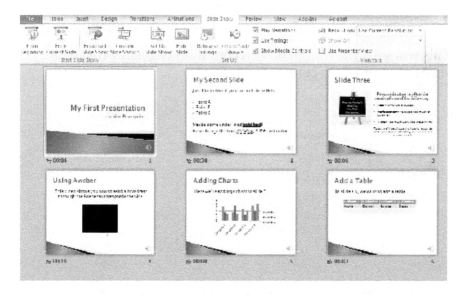

To preview your new recording, click the From Beginning play button at the top left of the navigation bar in the Slide Show ribbon. You can also press F5 on your keyboard. As you are previewing the show, look on the bottom left corner. You will see some navigation buttons and other buttons with which to edit the slides.

There is a left arrow and a right arrow so you can go forward or back with the presentation.

The pencil button will reveal this menu:

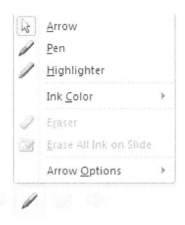

You can use these to draw on the presentation while it is running if you wish.

The next button will produce this menu:

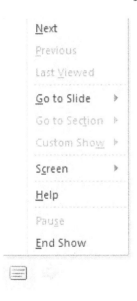

This will help you navigate through the slides, helping you spot any issues with your slide show so that you can edit it before you publish it.

Step 3: Check the Entire Slide Show

Run through the slideshow on presentation mode at least three times. Note down anything that needs to be changed, such as the slide show transitions, timing, and so on.

Hit the Escape button if you want to stop the show and tweak anything that you spot. Then play it back from the start, or from that particular slide.

Step 4: Publish your Presentation

When you are completely satisfied with your presentation, it will be time to publish it. Click the File tab, then Info. Here you can set your permissions, optimize the video and more. These are optional, so you can skip this if you wish, but we will review your choices now so that you can be clear about them:

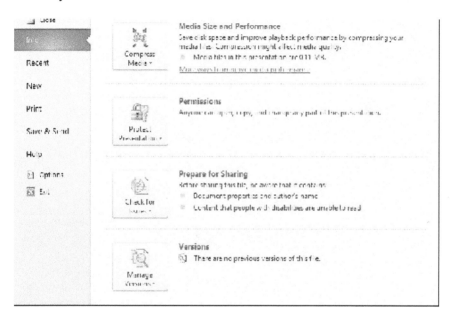

Media Size and Performance: This allows you to set the quality of your video. You can choose presentation quality, Internet quality or low quality, which would compress your files to save disk space, though it would lower the quality of the video, as the name suggests.

Permissions: If this file is meant to be viewed by only one person or a special group of people, you can set up permissions so that only those with the right information can access it.

Prepare for Sharing: This will check for any issues with your video. It also gives you the ability to change the properties on your presentation and notes, as well as adjust it for those with disabilities so they can also view the information.

Versions: You can revert back to previous versions by clicking on the ones which will be listed in this area.

Once you have made your selections, choose the Save and Send tab. Click Create a Video:

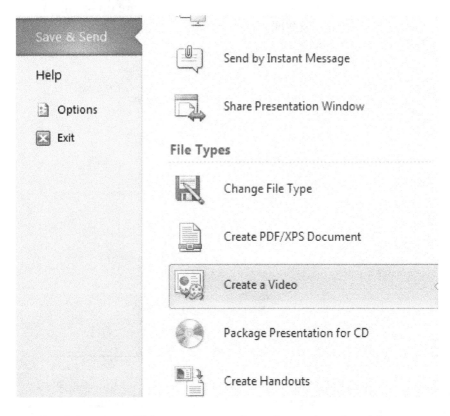

To the right, you will have some options for setting the video displays. Use the drop-down menu to make your selections:

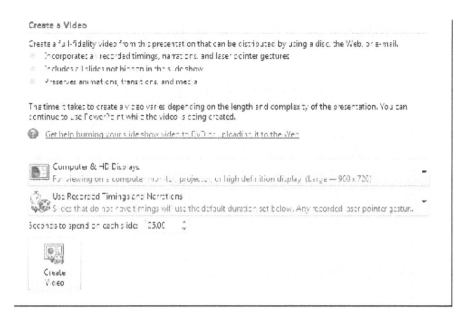

Here are the options when you open the drop-downs:

Computer and HD Displays

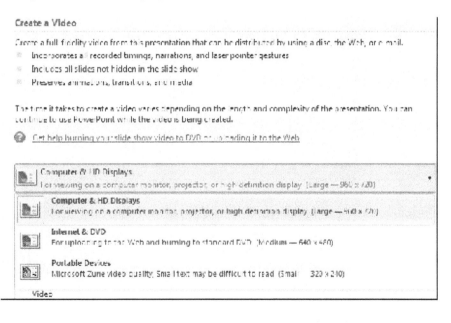

By default, the quality is set to Computer & HD Displays, which creates a movie at a 960×720 resolution and meant for viewing on a computer or burning to a DVD.

If you set the quality to Internet & DVD, it will be of medium quality with a resolution of 640×480.

The Portable Devices option is the lowest quality and has a 320×240 resolution.

Confirming the Timings:

This is a last-minute option to change the timings on the video. Most of the time, you would choose to use timings and narration you have already set up:

If you haven't set up the timings or want to make changes to the ones you have set up, turn this option off and enter the number of seconds you want to spend on each slide. Once you've made your selections, click the Create Video button and the save as dialog will pop up where you can name and save your video.

As you can see, you have a very wide variety of choices of format in which to save:

Presentation21.pptx ▼

PowerPoint Presentation (*.pptx) ▼

PowerPoint Presentation (*.pptx)
PowerPoint Macro-Enabled Presentation (*.pptm)
PowerPoint 97-2003 Presentation (*.ppt)
PDF (*.pdf)
XPS Document (*.xps)
PowerPoint Template (*.potx)
PowerPoint Macro-Enabled Template (*.potm)
PowerPoint 97-2003 Template (*.pot)
Office Theme (*.thmx)
PowerPoint Show (*.ppsx)
PowerPoint Macro-Enabled Show (*.ppsm)
PowerPoint 97-2003 Show (*.pps)
PowerPoint Add-In (*.ppam)
PowerPoint 97-2003 Add-In (*.ppa)
PowerPoint XML Presentation (*.xml)
Windows Media Video (*.wmv)
GIF Graphics Interchange Format (*.gif)
JPEG File Interchange Format (*.jpg)
PNG Portable Network Graphics Format (*.png)
TIFF Tag Image File Format (*.tif)
Device Independent Bitmap (*.bmp)
Windows Metafile (*.wmf)
Enhanced Windows Metafile (*.emf)
Outline/RTF (*.rtf)
PowerPoint Picture Presentation (*.pptx)
OpenDocument Presentation (*.odp)

but in this case, we are creating a video, so we would need to choose .wmv:

A Windows media video (.wmv) is a format that can be viewed by most people without needing PowerPoint.

Name your presentation and then click Save:

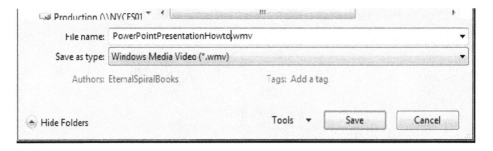

Now that your video is ready to go, you simply need to upload it to your website, YouTube, Facebook or wherever you want it to be displayed.

Since video files can be very large, the best way to keep them organized and stored safely is to upload them to YouTube, and then embed the code you will get once the file is published. If you don't wish everyone in the world to see the video, choose the Private or Unlisted feature. Close the comments if you don't want mad spammers or other crazies attacking your page.

If you need the video in another format, you will need a video converter. There are several free ones online that work well. Read the reviews at cnet.com and decide which one is right for your purposes depending upon the file you wish to create:

http://download.cnet.com/windows/presentation-software/?tag=bc

MP4 is a popular format. It is one of the default save settings in the 2013 version of PowerPoint.

Once you have converted the file to video, you can upload it in a variety of places to help promote your business effectively. (See our guides on Video Sharing Sites and YouTube Marketing for more information.)

Now that we have covered the essentials of creating PowerPoint presentations, it is time to look at how to create effective presentations in order to meet your business goals.

CHAPTER 5: TOP TIPS FOR GREAT POWERPOINT PRESENTATIONS

Thanks to the wonders of PowerPoint, almost anyone can create an attractive presentation in minutes for business or personal purposes (such as a photo album of their recent holiday), but not everyone is able to create an interesting presentation, or deliver one.

In-person presentations can be stressful and physically demanding, while online presentations can be a great way to get your message across, but might lack the human touch if you are not careful.

In this chapter, we want to give some of our top tips for creating effective PowerPoint presentations that will command attention live, or as a video.

* Choose an attractive theme in interesting colors.
This will set the mood of your whole presentation. Try to match your business colors if you are using the presentation for business purposes, and especially if you are marketing to viewers who might not know much about your company.

* Choose a white background, and black or very dark text.
This will make it easy for everyone to follow along on the slides without straining their eyes on screen or at the back of the room.

* Follow the 10/20/30 rule at conferences:
   10 slides
   20 minutes
   30-point font

As Joan always points out, when educating and informing, simplicity is best and you do not want to overrun your time. Even if you are scheduled for a full hour of speaking, 10 slides in 20 minutes leaves plenty of time for questions.

If you want to add to the information depending on your audience, have a few hidden slides that can give them more information, which you can then easily unhide and use. (Go to the Slide Show tab, choose the slide you wish to hide, and click Hide Slide. The slide will be excluded from the presentation you are delivering at the click of a mouse, but you can always click on the thumbnail to access it.) The 30-point font makes things easy to read, even for people at the back of the room; there is nothing more frustrating than sitting through a presentation in which you can't see anything.

* Use handouts as appropriate.
Consider printing handouts of the slides to give to attendees, or emailing the deck prior to the presentation so that people may print and bring it with them to take notes, if they wish.

* Use images to support, enlighten and entertain.
Your images should support your text and vice versa. Avoid using images as filler in your presentation.

* Use SmartArt to add visual interest and graphic depictions.
If you have a lot of list-like elements, use SmartArt to make them more visually appealing. Compare the rather dull list here:

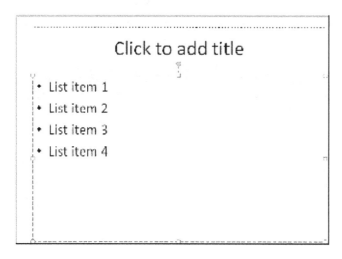

with this list:

Click to add title

List item 1

- List item 2 (or text related to the list item above)

List item 3

- List item 4 (or text related to the list item above)

The SmartArt adds color and interest to the slide and helps vary the slides in your deck even if you do not have many images.

* Use your animations and slide transitions wisely.
Do not use animations on every slide, and do not use silly ones at a serious business meeting.

* Use your animations and slide transitions in order to command attention and enhance meaning.
Make sure your transitions help command attention by using ones which help enhance meaning, such as introducing each bullet on the page with a click so that each bullet appears one at a time.

* Use the master slides and pre-prepared layouts to make everything look uniform.
There are several choices on the New Slide menu for pre-set slide templates. Use these to speed up the slide creation process and have everything organized in terms of fonts and color schemes:

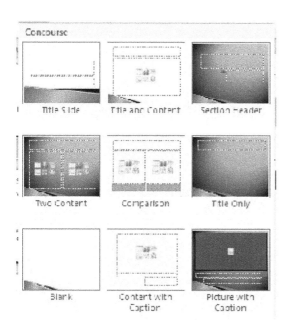

Concourse

Title Slide Title and Content Section Header

Two Content Comparison Title Only

Blank Content with Picture with
              Caption   Caption

* Add a footer with your logo to make everything look uniform. Your URL and logo would both be good choices from a branding perspective.

* Add slide numbers to your slides if you do not plan to hide slides. If the presentation is short, number the slides. If you think you will not use the whole deck, leave out the numbers.

* Avoid creating presentations with very large file sizes. Compress your images, and do not overdo it with audio or video. If you plan to share your presentation at top video sharing websites such as YouTube, keep the file size under 10 MB and a run time of fewer than 9 minutes. The secret with most video sharing sites is to create a channel with regularly-scheduled video releases, in the same way that television stations set programming for their viewers.

* Proofread and check everything. Review your presentation several times for errors. Also check that the animations and transitions are working the way you wish them to.

* Use the outline and note features to help keep you organized.

If you are giving the presentation in person, use the outline and notes to help you stay organized under pressure. It is easy to miss an important point if you are nervous, or if you are having any technical issues. You can access the outline view on the left-hand pane and the notes in the window pane under each slide where it says "Click to add notes." Don't forget to look at your notes and print them using various views to help keep yourself organized.

* Test and rehearse.
Test the presentation on a number of viewers and rehearse in front of a mirror, or some family and friends, until you can deliver your presentation with ease. Even if you are only narrating for video, your oral presentation should be clear, audible, and interest them through varied tones of voice. Avoid sounding as if you are reading from your notes. We sat on a dreadful investment webinar recently during which the person read over their notes in such a rushed way, it was all garbled, and then left 40 minutes for questions. So also be aware of pace and timing.

* Track and test your results.
Use the feedback you get to improve your presentation for the next time. If it is an in-house presentation, you might also be able to refine and improve it. If you think it is a good marketing tool without too much in-house information, consider turning it into a video and sharing it on one of the top slide sharing websites. (See Appendix 2 for more information.)

CHAPTER 6: TOP MARKETING USES FOR POWERPOINT PRESENTATIONS

PowerPoint presentations are attractive and interactive whether seen in person or at an online webinar. They are a great way to make what can be dry and dull information into a lively and colorful presentation with just a few clicks.

They can also be a great substitute for having to do a lot of writing if you do not have time, or are a great speaker but not much of a writer. With a few bullet points, images and captions, and some animations and transitions to liven things up, you can create a great marketing tool, even an ebook, in which people will be interested and perhaps even pass around.

Depending upon your business goals, you might use the presentation or video to launch a new product, or you might wish to sell the presentation as a webinar, on a DVD, as part of a course pack, or as part of a membership website related to your particular niche.

You can use presentations for coaching (see our guide on the subject), mentoring, and even brand exposure for your business. Putting a presentation up on a popular video sharing website and presentation site can be two of the best ways to get discovered by people who tend to be more visual in their learning style and do not want to plow through lots of writing to get to the essence of a subject.

Videos can be included on your website, at your blog, or in your email marketing. Send your newsletter subscribers the link to your latest video.

Embed your shared videos in your LinkedIn profile, and post them on Facebook and Pinterest. Then tweet about them, and perhaps in one of the top social networking websites, your video will be of such interest that it will go viral, that is, get spread around by your followers. If you have 100 followers, and each one of them tells two people, and those people tell two other people, you can see how fast your presentation can spread, and thus serve as a valuable marketing tool for your business.

PowerPoint presentations turned into video are also perfect for people who do not like to appear in front of a camera or are shy about being on stage. They are entertaining, but also educational in nature, allowing you to present factual information in an interesting way.

Joan's first use of a PowerPoint-like program many years ago was to teach students and to create multimedia and interactive presentations to review their literature texts, so she could be sure no one missed any important material if they were out sick. She now uses PowerPoint for instructional purposes, creating outlines for her ebooks which people can use as workbooks to remind themselves of the most essential skills they have learned.

No matter what industry or career you are currently working in, presentations can help you convey your message, give more brand exposure, and enable you to go viral on the social networks, provided that you have something interesting and even exciting to show your target audience.

You can also use your presentations as premium content, exclusive to your inner circle, or to those who can afford to pay for the presentation.

Webinars are one of the best ways to get new people into that inner circle by showing what you have to offer in order to make more sales. (See our guide on hosting successful webinars for more information.) Pre-recording the presentation for the webinar and creating great special offers for your products, plus surprise bonuses and a gift just for attending your online presentation, can be one of the best ways to create buzz for your business.

Recording your webinar or presentation and turning it into short videos for YouTube and other top video-sharing websites can be one of the best ways to get discovered and develop a whole new audience to market to. Once visitors come to your site, give them a reason to register, such as to access the whole of your presentation; once you have them on your email list, you can market to them on a regular basis.

Information publishing online is growing into a multi-billion dollar industry. If you do not already have streams of income flowing into your business related to ebooks, ecourses and so on, now is the time to master PowerPoint and begin using the presentations that you create as both a marketing tool and as product in their own right, free or paid, that can help you expand your business empire.

CONCLUSION

Evelyn can remember the height of the dot-com boom when people who were able to use PowerPoint were commanding $100 an hour. A quick search on a popular job board shows the current rate of pay at about $50 to $60, not bad for a program that is easy to use once you know how.

PowerPoint is like any of the other Microsoft Office programs: full of a lot of features and menus that can sometimes be confusing. The advantage of the Office suite programs, however, is that many of the menus have a lot in common from one program to the next. As Evelyn always tells people, if you can use Word or Excel, you can use PowerPoint. There are also free templates, clip art and more, which can also add to your marketing and presentation skills and the branding of your business across all of the marketing communication (marcom) items you create.

If you can write a good blog post with about five to ten brief, essential points, you can also create a PowerPoint presentation in the same way. Think about the needs of your target audience, and create and deliver laser-focused presentations full of information and interesting visuals. Then transform your presentations into ebooks, presentations, webinars and videos, all at the touch of a couple of buttons.

With online information publishing booming and online education becoming even more popular, both formal and informal, you can transform your PowerPoint presentations into profit powerhouses by using them as both marketing tools, and products for sale in their own right.

For your convenience, we have summarized the main steps to create a deck in Appendix 1. We have also created a special page for you to download this checklist of action steps to create your presentations here:

http://eternalspiralbooks.com/ppp
password: presentwell

In Appendix 2, discover why you should publish your decks on SlideShare, and how to get started. Use the Further Reading Suggestions for more marketing information for beginners to fill in any gaps you might have with reference to marketing your business successfully online using your great decks as the basis for success.

We wish you the best of success with marketing and sales from your new PowerPoint presentations.

JM
ET
December 4. 2016

FURTHER READING

Please visit the Marketing Matters page for the latest Marketing for small business titles.
http://eternalspiralbooks.com/category/categories-series/marketing-matters/

APPENDIX 1: CHECKLIST TO CREATE A POWERPOINT PRESENTATION

Top tips for creating effective PowerPoint presentations that will command attention live, or as a video:

1-Choose an attractive theme in interesting colors.

2-Choose a white background, and black or very dark text.

3-Follow the 10/20/30 rule at conferences:
  10 slides
  20 minutes
  30-point font

4-Use handouts as appropriate.

5-Use images to support, enlighten and entertain.

6-Use SmartArt to add visual interest and graphic depictions.

7-Use your animations and slide transitions wisely.

8-Use your animations and slide transitions in order to command attention and enhance meaning.

9-Use the master slides and pre-prepared layouts to make everything look uniform.

10-Add a footer with your logo to make everything look uniform.

11-Add slide numbers to your slides if you do not plan to hide slides.

12-Avoid creating presentations with very large file sizes.

13-Proofread and check everything.

14-Use the outline and note features to help keep you organized.

15-Test and rehearse.

16-Track and test your results.

APPENDIX 2: HOW TO ADD A SLIDE SHOW TO SLIDESHARE

Thanks to the popularity of YouTube, which has created a trend for sharing videos, people online have also discovered the value of viewing great slideshows from top businesses and marketers.

Slideshows provide useful information for all types of consumers, from business to consumer (B2C), business to business (B2B), and business to an educational audience (B2E). Many people learn in a visual way, and a good slideshow can be even more interesting than the best-written blog post, and on a par with a good video. Slide shows are not just a learning tool, however. They are also a great way for a business owner to provide value and promote their business. Slideshows marry visual content with text for powerful marketing messages.

What Is SlideShare?

SlideShare is the world's largest community for sharing presentations. It has recently been purchased by LinkedIn, so you can be sure your business or marketing presentation will get much higher visibility and you can link to it easily from your profile, and vice versa. It is free to use and offers more than just slide shows. Users can also upload documents, PDFs, videos and webinars.

While there is some fun content, the majority of it is professional content, including presentations, infographics, documents, and videos. Sharing content on SlideShare can build your reputation as a thought-leader in your niche and cultivate more professional opportunities.

This would be a convenient tool for those reasons alone, but it has other convenient features as well.
For example, when you upload the deck, it will produce a transcript at the bottom that is full of keywords to attract an audience to your deck.

The embed code means you can add it to your site or WordPress blog with just a couple of clicks. SlideShare offers an abundance of business-building possibilities that you should take advantage of sooner rather than later.

How to Add a Slide Show to SlideShare

Step 1: Sign up at the website

Visit SlideShare and sign up for your free account. Remember to use your business rather than your personal information. You will need to create a username and add an email. You also have the choice to link your slide shows with your social media accounts. If you have not built out full account profiles at LinkedIn and Facebook, you might wish to take a few moments to do this. If your content is highly visual, build out a Pinterest profile as well. Remember that all your profiles should be consistent with the brand or business you are trying to build, and with your marketing goals.

Step 2: Upload your slide show

Once you have signed up for your SlideShare account, you will see an Upload option at the top of the page. Click Upload and you can then add your deck by dragging and dropping, or searching for it on your computer. It is important to know the formats you can add. They include:
* Presentations: PDF, PowerPoint, OpenOffice, Apple Keynote
* Documents: PDF, doc, docx, rtf, OpenOffice, Apple iWork Pages, txt, csv

Their What to Upload page videos can give you more information and inspiration. http://www.slideshare.net/ss/creators/get-started As you can see, you can upload just about any presentation software or document type available. However, the file size limit for a single presentation is 100 MB.

They have recently added a feature that allows you to collect business leads from your decks. This is ideal for email marketing to the leads you get. https://www.slideshare.net/lead-campaigns/new You can view more details here: http://www.slideshare.net/ss/creators/for-businesses?from=sub-nav

It is important to pay attention to the terms of service on SlideShare. You cannot upload materials for which you do not hold the copyright. Only upload decks that you have created yourself, with your own images or those you are certain are in the public domain, such as at Wikimedia Commons. Be sure your content will not violate anyone else's copyright in any way.

If you have a niche that lends itself to a slide show form of information, consider signing up for SlideShare and help those slide shows reach more prospects. You should soon see a steady stream of people interested in your niche who will be eager to learn more about all you have to offer coming to your website through SlideShare.

FREE NEWSLETTER OFFER

Please visit us online at Eternal Spiral Books for a free newsletter packed full of special members-only discounts, articles, guides and more: http://EternalSpiralBooks.com/newsletter

www.ingramcontent.com/pod-product-compliance
Lightning Source LLC
Chambersburg PA
CBHW052149070326
40689CB00050B/2525